Sam is fed up.
Mouse and Jojo are away
on holiday. So is Ben.

1

Sam gets postcards from them.

SCOTLAND

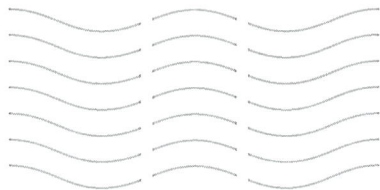

Dear Sam,

I have seen a Highland cow.

Love,

Ben

Sam Summerday,
Flat 4B,
Story Court,
Wellbridge
WB4 HP4

1ST

4

TUNISIA

Dear Sam,

We have seen
a camel.

Love,

Mouse and Jojo

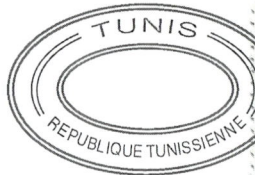

Sam Summerday,
Flat 4B,
Story Court,
Wellbridge
WB4 HP4

REPUBLIQUE TUNISIENNE

الجمهورية التونسية
زهرالأكاسيا
FLEURS D'ACACIA

Acacia cyanophilla Lindl.

ALI FAKHET   POSTES   البريد   **70**   1999

TUNIS

REPUBLIQUE TUNISSIENNE

6

"I wish I could see
a Highland cow," says Sam.
"I wish I could see a camel."

Sam's mum
has an idea.

The Wellbridge News

'T PIANO

A day at
WELLBRIDGE

ANIMAL WORLD

FREE!

Just take this
token from the
Wellbridge News

They go to Animal World.
Sam sees lots of animals.

When it is time to go,
Sam has an idea.

ANIMAL

11

Dear Ben,

I have seen a Highland cow too!

Love,

Sam

Ben King,
31 Story Street,
Wellbridge
WB4 HS2

2ND

12

WELLBRIDGE
ANIMAL WORLD

13

Dear Mouse
and Jojo,

I have seen
a camel too!

Love,

Sam

Mouse and Jojo
Macdonald,
30 Story Street,
Wellbridge
WB4 HS2

"What was the best part of the day?" asks Mum.

"Sending the postcards!" says Sam.